Ponies
For Kids

Amazing Animal Books
For Young Readers

By
Rachel Smith

Mendon Cottage Books

JD-Biz Publishing

Read More Amazing Animal Books

Purchase at Amazon.com

Table of Contents

Introduction

Ponies are the pet that many girls and boys long for. They are in TV shows and movies, in books and on stickers. But what exactly is the animal like, and what makes a pony a pony?

They actually have long had use in many parts of the world not always as a beloved pet, but as a work horse. Ponies are strong, and they are used by many different peoples, from Tibetans to the British.

As an animal, they are easier to take care of than horses in some ways. For instance, they consume less food than horses; they are also not able to jump as high.

Ponies have been around for almost as long as any nation can remember. Ponies were ridden by Eurasian Steppe peoples (such as the Huns or Mongols) and they have long been kept by both nomad peoples and sedentary (meaning people who live in one place, such as a city or a farm) peoples.

The pony is a staple of the farm around the world, and if ponies had not existed, those at the corners of civilization would have had a much harder time getting by.

What are ponies?

If you define ponies by an easy definition, it's that they are 14.2 hands high and no taller. Horses and ponies are both measured by hands rather than feet, and a full grown horse will typically be much bigger than a pony.

A horse and a pony playing.

Ponies are also differently shaped than horses. They have more barrel-shaped bodies, shorter legs, thick necks and short heads, and heavier, tougher bones. They also grow a thicker coat than horses, because of where they tend to live.

They were made to survive in places that would be harder for a horse to survive; that's why they're smaller. There was less to eat where ponies developed, so they developed in a different way than other horses.

Technically, any small horse can be called a pony, but most ponies are like they have been described above. If it's for an official competition, then a pony absolutely has to be 14.2-14.2 ½ hands high or less.

Ponies are a type of horse. Every pony is a horse, but not every horse is a pony.

A male pony is called a stallion; a male pony who can't have babies is called a gelding. Female ponies are called mares; baby horses are called foals. Male ponies under four years are called colts, while females under four years are called fillies. Lastly, a yearling is a pony that is between one and two years old.

What do ponies eat?

Ponies eat the same things horses eat, just less of it. Digestion for ponies begins in the mouth, with saliva helping to break down food. Their prehensile lips are well designed for picking up roughage (or plants, such as prairie grass).

Horses, and ponies, need protein for growth, as it's the building block of the body. Ponies don't get protein from meat like many animals do; they it from legumes, which are a plant type of food packed with protein. Alfalfa is an example of a protein rich food that ponies eat.

Ponies also need fat and carbohydrates. This is where they get their energy, in a similar way to humans.

They can eat roughage, as well as grains and foods that are in the shape of pellets. Lots of horses nowadays have feed, rather than relying solely on grazing.

Ponies get overweight more easily from too much food. It's very important that they are fed what they need and no more. Also, if they are given too much energy food, they can become restless and harder to ride.

Also, ponies need a diet high in fiber (which helps digest food, among other things) and less sugars and starches than a horse. Ponies will usually need less supplements (things added to their diet) than a horse, because they are hardier and lived in areas with less food when they were wild.

Water is very important in a pony's diet; most will only last a few days without water.

How do ponies act?

Ponies will spend most of their day eating small amounts. Their digestive systems are designed to take in small amounts of food at a time, though the horse eats far more often than humans' three meals a day.

Two ponies playing in a pasture.

Ponies also enjoy playing. They will nip at each other, chase each other, and just enjoy a good romp around the pasture. Ponies are not lazy creatures, though they need a strong hand to raise them right.

A pony can be stubborn and willful, as compared to a regular horse, though most of the time this happens due to improper training. One that has been properly trained is perfect for children to ride, and a large pony can carry an adult.

Many breeds of ponies are much gentler to children than a full size horse. They tend to be more laid back than a full size horse, though some can be quite a lot of trouble.

Ponies were mostly used as draft animals, so ponies have been bred to be very strong. They can do more work than a draft horse (a horse bred to do things like pull a plow or a cart), and as mentioned before, they eat much less. This makes them a very good choice for working on a farm.

They are known for being more cunning than most horses, meaning that they figure out things more easily, such as escaping from their pens. That said, they are some of the more friendly animals out there.

Miniature horses versus ponies

Miniature horses are small horses. However, they are not ponies; they would almost be too small to be a real pony.

A black miniature horse.

Miniature horses have a very similar build to a regular horse; the only difference is size. Miniature horses can be as small as 34 inches and smaller.

They are usually smaller than ponies, but during the 1800's, they were used for some of the same purposes: carrying things out of mines. They were used as packhorses.

However, a key difference would be that miniature horses were often kept as pets by the nobility; most miniature horses can't be ridden on due to their size. They were very interesting to the nobility, and so they were kept on like so many other marvels.

There is also a difference between miniature horses and dwarf horses. Dwarf horses tend to hold the records for smallest horses, but that's because they have a condition similar to that of human dwarves; their legs are short and stubby, as compared to a miniature horse, whose legs are fairly long compared to their body.

Dwarf horses would not be small if it weren't for the mutation of a gene, generally speaking. Miniature horses are naturally small, and their bodies are identical to normal sized horses.

A miniature horse without anything next to it to give away its size should be easily mistaken for a normal horse in a picture.

Miniature horses are also used as service animals, like a blind person's seeing-eye dog. Some visit children in hospitals too.

Shetland ponies

Shetland ponies are one of the better known kinds of ponies. They come from a place called the Shetland Isles; it's a subarctic (nearly up near the North Pole!) place just off of Britain.

A Shetland pony.

Shetland ponies are particularly short, only going up to about 11 hands tall. They have short legs, and large barrel-shaped bodies. They are very stocky, and their hair grows in a double coat for winter, because it gets so cold on the Shetland Isles.

They are very gentle ponies, and very sweet-natured. They make an ideal mount for a child, unlike some more lively breeds of horse or pony. They are also the strongest horse or pony for their size. If the load is double its weight, it can often still pull it.

They have been on the Shetland Isles since about the Bronze Age, which was thousands of years ago.

Before the Industrial Revolution (when machines were used for many things), the Shetland pony stayed on the Shetland Isles and was used for things like farmwork. However, when there were many mines that needed ponies, many of them were shipped off to Britain. Some were even sent to the United States.

However, after that had passed, Shetland ponies became popular as pets. They were kept on farms and other places, instead of the horrible conditions of the mines.

A registry was started to keep track of the pony breed, and ever since then, Shetland ponies have been in shows for horses and ponies.

Like the miniature horse, Shetland ponies have also been trained to be guide animals, like guide dogs. Since they are so small, they can go in most places and help their disabled owners. However, they must be miniature Shetland ponies, or else they will be too big to get into most places safely.

Most of the time, however, Shetland ponies are ridden by children for fun. They aren't big enough to hold most adults, because they are so small.

They are also involved in harness racing, though still only ridden by children about ages 6-16.

Welsh ponies

Welsh ponies have been around for a long time. Since they are descended from Welsh mountain ponies, they are very hardy; they used to run wild through Britain, especially in Wales, which is a part of the United Kingdom.

A Welsh pony.

Welsh ponies were bred with Arabian horses sometime after the Romans showed up in Britain. However, they still kept most of the things that made them Welsh ponies and not Arabian horses.

At one point, the Welsh pony was in danger, because King Henry VIII of England (and Wales) declared that all horses under a certain height must be put to death; he only wanted big horses for his army. However, his daughter, Queen Elizabeth I, repealed (undid) the decree, because she found it was too hard on the poor peasants to kill so many horses and ponies.

The Welsh pony has a pretty mixed blood. Many different horses, Arabians included, crossbred with them, so they will never be quite like they were before foreign forces showed up in the land.

They love to go fast, and they can be hard to keep under control. However, they make excellent pets for people interested in keeping ponies. They also have small heads, big eyes, and very powerful legs.

Often, this type of pony was used for mailmen to deliver the mail with. They were also used in mines, and for other uses as packhorses.

Chinese Guoxia ponies

Chinese Guoxia ponies are very small. They are usually only up to 10 hands high, making them around the size of miniature horses.

This type of pony is descended from the Mongolian horse, the forerunner of many different horses in the East Asia area (Mongolia, China, Korea, etc.). Most horses descended from the Mongolian horse are rather small, but most aren't considered ponies.

The Chinese Guoxia pony has a large, heavy head, and short ears. They are best at pulling things with harnesses, and they make good children's ponies.

At one point, this pony was thought to be extinct, until around 1981 when a revival of the breed was started. It is a very old breed, possibly from longer than 2,000 years ago.

A Chinese Guoxia pony is considered a pony due to the way it is built: a lot like prehistoric horses, with a big head and shorter legs.

Fell ponies

Fell ponies are a type of pony from England. They come from the north, where there are moorlands and mountains.

A fell pony mare with her foal.

They are very strong, hardworking ponies. Since fell ponies were bred for a very harsh environment (place they live), they can live almost anywhere. They are hardy, and surefooted, since they live in mountains.

Fell ponies are usually black; they used to have about half brown, far back when the records were first kept on them, but since then black has become the dominant color.

They were used as packhorses. They carried things like slate and copper, all the way up past the beginning of the 20th century.

They are mostly used for riding nowadays; fells come in all sizes, so some can carry adults and others can carry children.

Fell ponies were very popular among the Vikings who settled in England; they used them a lot.

For a while, fell pony numbers went down; then, around 1945, breeding programs were started in England for all types of ponies and horses. The fifties also helped, as more people had money for horses to keep just for riding, rather than for work.

Miyako ponies

Miyako uma Haidonan Wikimedia Commons

Miyako ponies are very rare. There are only roughly twenty left in the world.

They come from Japan, and are a very old breed. Like the Chinese Guoxia pony, they are related to the Mongolian horse, and are fairly small.

They tend to be tan. These ponies were used as draft animals, though nowadays they are watched a lot more closely, since there's only a handful of them left.

The reason for the smaller number of ponies is simple: with new things for work such as cars, trucks, and tractors, the pony wasn't needed anymore. It went from thousands in the 1950's to its present tiny number.

Miyako ponies are mainly kept for riding nowadays, and sometimes work around a farm.

It is one of only eight breeds native to Japan.

Tibetan ponies

The Tibetan pony is a name belonging to a group of about six breeds native to Tibet. Scientists are not sure if they descended from Mongolian horses like the Miyako pony and the Chinese Guoxia pony, or if they are their own pure breed from Tibet.

A Tibetan pony. by **Kersti Nebelsiek** Wikimedia Commons

This type of pony has been around for a very long time. They are usually used as pack horses; in fact, they've been used as pack horses for tea for so long that one of the roads they traveled for hundreds of years is called the Tea-Horse Road.

These ponies were often traded for things as well. They are very surefooted animals, because of the terrain (land) in Tibet.

They have also been crossbred with other ponies to make new kinds of ponies, such as the Indian Country Bred.

Tibetan ponies were not typically used for nomads, but for a sedentary community, unlike the Mongolian horse that some think they descended from.

Quarter ponies

Quarter ponies are the small version of quarter horses; at the very least, they were bred from the same stock. It is specifically bred to look like a small version of a quarter horse.

A quarter pony.

Quarter ponies came about from small quarter horses, a breed prominent in America. They can come in many different colors and patterns.

Unlike a lot of other ponies, quarter ponies are mainly used for riding, and don't have a long history of being used as pack animals. They have long been show horses as well.

Since they are significantly newer than a lot of ponies, quarter ponies have several guidelines to identify them as quarter ponies. Three different organizations exist that all have different ideas of what a quarter pony should look like, but they all have similar guidelines: a quarter pony must look like a quarter horse, but be under 14.2 hands high.

Interestingly, the rule used to be that a quarter horse under 14.2 hands high was disqualified to present as a quarter horse, and that's what led to the breed of quarter ponies; however, even though that's been changed, quarter ponies are still going strong.

Kerry bog ponies

Kerry bog ponies come from Ireland, in County Kerry. They were wild at first, living among the bogs and marshes; then, the Irish tamed them and they became working horses for farms.

A young Kerry bog pony. Tsaag Valren Wikimedia Commons

Because Kerry bog ponies' weight compared to their height is light, they can walk on wet ground without sinking in. Typically, Kerry bog ponies are about 10-12 hands high, making them a bit shorter than some other ponies. Mares are often smaller than the stallions.

The interesting thing about Kerry bog ponies is that the Irish didn't keep them in pastures or penned in; in earlier times, they were simply turned loose in the bogs and then caught again when they were needed. This way, the Irish, who were mostly poor farmers, didn't have to feed them.

Since Kerry bog ponies were adapted to living in bogs, they almost never ended up sinking. This was also the place that they would mate and have foals.

Because of war (the British would take the Irish's ponies and use them as packhorses, and then never return them) and the change from small farms to machines, the number of Kerry bog ponies fell. Soon, they were nearly extinct; it was only in the 1990's that it was made an official and an organization was founded that helped make sure the breed didn't die out.

It is only due to the work of this organization that the Kerry bog pony is still around; they were lucky to find about 20 ponies left to breed for a new stock.

Mongolian horses

Mongolian horses, also known as Mongol horses, have been around for as far back as humans can remember; they are the forerunners of many different horses and ponies in the East Asia area.

A Mongolian nomad and his Mongol horse.

Despite being small, Mongolian horses are not ponies. They are stocky, with big heads, yet they have not been classified as ponies.

Mongolian horses are used typically by the Mongolian people. Since thousands of years ago, the Mongols rode these horses for everything from traveling to herding their animals to warfare.

Most Mongolians nowadays can ride a horse; in their history, they were mostly nomads (meaning that they didn't stay in one place very long), and horses were important for a lifestyle like that.

Mongolian horses are used nowadays for carrying things, being ridden, and for horse races. Most of the time, a Mongolian horse will canter, which is not a run. However, for races, they will go full speed with children as their jockeys. This type of horse is usually trained to keep running even if their jockey falls off!

This type of horse has changed very little since 2000 BC. Perhaps it is because they are a very good fit for their job, and the Mongolians don't care to breed them into a different form.

Conclusion

Ponies are amazing around the world. They are found on most continents (Antarctica being one obvious exception), and have filled in where normal horses could not.

They have also given great pleasure to children, because a pony is mostly a child's horse. Thousands upon thousands of children have ridden ponies throughout history, and they will continue to ride as long as ponies are around.

Ponies are great starter horses; they are perfect for teaching a child to ride. They are also in the dreams of children everywhere. There are few children who would not want a pony for Christmas, their birthday, or another gift-giving occasion.

The pony may be underrepresented, but it is a charming animal, from its typically gentle nature to the great intelligence it tends to show. Ponies are the ones who will figure out a way out of their pasture or pen; they are wily, all while being as sweet as a rabbit or a well-loved dog.

Author Bio

Rachel Smith is a young author who enjoys animals. She's always wanted to get a both a guinea pig and a rabbit and have them live together. Once, she had a rabbit who was very nervous, and chewed through her leash and tried to escape. She's also had several pet mice, who were the funniest little animals to watch. Ponies are one of her favorite kinds of animals, and she's ridden a couple. She lives in Ohio with her family and writes in her spare time.

Our books are available at

1. Amazon.com

2. Barnes and Noble

3. Itunes

4. Kobo

5. Smashwords

6. Google Play Books

This book is published by

JD-Biz Corp

P O Box 374

Mendon, Utah 84325

http://www.jd-biz.com/

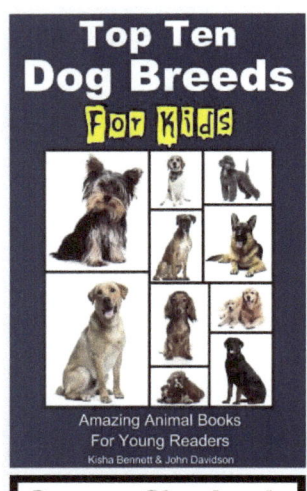

Top Ten Dog Breeds For Kids

Amazing Animal Books For Young Readers
Kisha Bennett & John Davidson

Poodles

Dog Books for Kids
K. Bennett

Labrador Retrievers

Dog Books for Kids
K. Bennett

German Shepherds

Dog Books for Kids
K. Bennett

Rottweilers

Dog Books for Kids
K. Bennett

Boxers

Dog Books for Kids
K. Bennett

Golden Retrievers

Dog Books for Kids
K. Bennett

Beagles

Dog Books for Kids
K. Bennett

Yorkies

Dog Books for Kids
K. Bennett